P9-DMH-087

★ ★ ★ IT'S MY STATE! ★ ★ ★

OKLAHOMA

Doug Sanders

Geoffrey M. Horn

Cavendish
Square
New York

Published in 2014 by Cavendish Square Publishing, LLC
303 Park Avenue South, Suite 1247, New York, NY 10010

Website: cavendishsq.com

This publication represents the opinions and views of the authors based on their personal experience, knowledge, and research. The information in this book serves as a general guide only. The authors and publisher have used their best efforts in preparing this book and disclaim liability rising directly or indirectly from the use and application of this book.

CPSIA Compliance Information: Batch #WS13CSQ

All websites were available and accurate when this book was sent to press.

Library of Congress Cataloging-in-Publication Data

Sanders, Doug, 1972-
       Oklahoma / Doug Sanders, Geoffrey M. Horn. — 2nd ed.
          p. cm. — (It's my state!)
       Summary: "Surveys the history, geography, government, economy, and people of Oklahoma"—Provided by publisher.
       Includes bibliographical references and index.
       ISBN 978-0-7614-8001-3 (hardcover) —ISBN 978-1-62712-102-6 (paperback)— ISBN 978-0-7614-8008-2 (ebook)
       1. Oklahoma—Juvenile literature. I. Horn, Geoffrey M. II. Title.
F694.3.S26 2014
976.6—dc23
                                2012024135

This edition developed for Cavendish Square Publishing by RJF Publishing LLC (www.RJFpublishing.com)
Series Designer, Second Edition: Tammy West/Westgraphix LLC

OKLAHOMA

CONTENTS

State Tree: Redbud

In spring, the redbud's clusters of pinkish flowers often bloom before the heart-shaped leaves appear. The redbud became the official tree in 1937, prompting one poet to write: "And this is Oklahoma's tree of loveliness so rare, / A symbol of red earth and free, when blooming anywhere."

State Floral Emblem: Mistletoe

Although mistletoe is not really a flower, it became an official territorial symbol in 1893, before Oklahoma was even a state. Mistletoe lives on trees that grow across the state. The dark green leaves and white berries of the plant are a common sight in Oklahoma in fall and winter.

State Bird: Scissor-Tailed Flycatcher

This bird almost missed its chance to be an official state symbol. In a vote sponsored by the Oklahoma Federation of Women's Clubs in 1929, students chose the bobwhite as the state bird, but the state legislature did not follow the recommendation. Instead, in May 1951, the flycatcher was officially adopted. It is known for its extremely long black-and-white tail, as well as for the elaborate "sky dance" it performs to attract a mate.

State Reptile: Collared Lizard

Oklahoma's collared lizards can frequently be seen sunning themselves in the Wichita Mountains. Early white settlers in the region nicknamed this silent reptile "mountain boomer," because they believed it was responsible for loud noises they were hearing. The settlers probably heard the loud calls of frogs and mistakenly thought that collared lizards were the source.

State Animal: Bison

The bison (also known as the buffalo) became the state animal in 1972. Long before Oklahoma became a state, millions of bison roamed the Great Plains region. By the 1890s, fewer than 1,000 remained. As a result, concerned citizens began to protect this important American animal. Today, bison can be found in Oklahoma parks and wildlife sanctuaries, and on the open plains. More than 200 farms and ranches in the state raise bison for meat.

State Butterfly: Black Swallowtail

As a caterpillar, this insect sports a vibrant pattern of white, black, and green stripes with rows of yellow dots. As a butterfly, the swallowtail is mostly black with bands or spots of yellow. Adults flit along the fields and roadsides of Oklahoma, drawing the nectar from plants such as red clover, milkweed, and thistle.

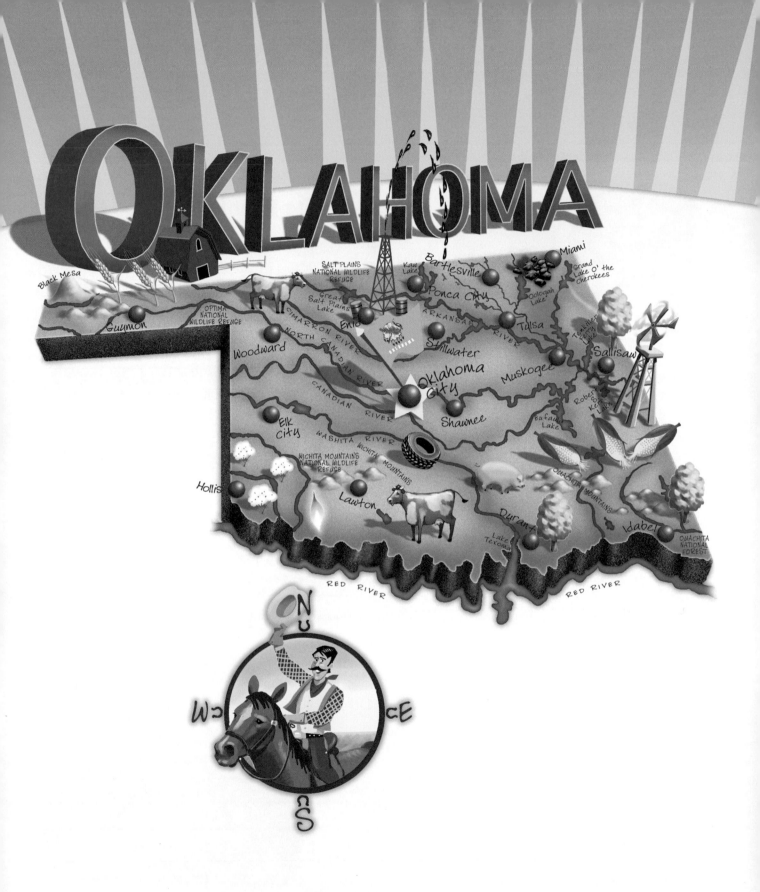

The Sooner State

Oklahoma's land is as varied as its people. The state, which covers 77 counties, mostly consists of a massive rolling plain. It slopes gently downward as it unfolds from northwest to southeast. Those two compass points mark the two extremes of the state's geography and climate. The state's highest point is Black Mesa, near the border with New Mexico and Colorado. At 4,973 feet (1,516 meters), Oklahoma's highest point offers great views of the surrounding area. The mesa—which is a small, isolated hill with steep sides—was created millions of years ago when lava oozed out of a nearby volcano and then hardened. The mesa is located at the northwest tip of the Oklahoma Panhandle. The Panhandle is a strip of land 166 miles (267 kilometers) long and 34 miles (55 km) wide. As its name suggests, it looks like a handle that is sticking out of the state's northwestern corner.

Oklahoma's lowest point in elevation is found in the southeast, at the opposite corner of the state. Near Idabel, close to the border with Texas and Arkansas, the land dips to 289 feet (88 m) above sea level. The eastern region of the state, along the border with Arkansas and Missouri, is the most heavily forested part

Quick Facts

OKLAHOMA BORDERS

North	Colorado
	Kansas
South	Texas
East	Arkansas
	Missouri
West	Texas
	New Mexico

Dinosaur tracks made tens of millions of years ago can be seen in a creek bed near Black Mesa in the Oklahoma Panhandle.

of Oklahoma. About one-sixth of the state is covered in trees, and many are found clustered in the east.

Eastern Oklahoma

Eastern Oklahoma is a region of flat, fertile plains and low hills. One of the most notable features is the Ozark Plateau. A plateau is a stretch of raised land with a nearly level surface. The Ozark Plateau extends into the state from nearby Missouri and Arkansas. Residents often refer to this part of the state as Oklahoma's Green Country. Clear, swift-flowing rivers and streams help keep the area lush. The waters flow through steep-walled valleys, which break up the wide stretches of flat-topped uplands. The rivers helped create these valleys and the high bluffs that often line the banks. Over millions of years, the water's flow slowly carved these trenches into the land.

The southeastern part of Oklahoma is well forested and supports an active lumber industry. The region is also home to the Ouachitas, one of the state's few mountain chains. The Ouachitas consist

The natural beauty of the Ouachita National Forest, located partly in Oklahoma and partly in Arkansas, attracts hikers, campers, and other visitors.

of groups of tall sandstone ridges that stretch from west to east. The Ouachitas make up one of the most rugged regions in the state. Natural springs bubble up, and sparkling streams course in and out of the many valleys tucked between the ridges.

Between the Ozark Plateau and the Ouachitas is the region known as the Prairie Plains. Crops thrive in this part of Oklahoma, which is flat and mostly treeless. East of Muskogee, the Arkansas River valley is an especially fertile part of the state. Much of the state's coal and major pockets of petroleum are also found there.

Central Oklahoma

Like the eastern region, Central Oklahoma features a variety of landscapes. Starting on the northern edge of the state, near the border with Kansas, sandstone hills rise 250 to 400 feet (75 to 120 m) high. Many of the hills are lined with flowering blackjack plants and with post oaks and other types of trees. The sandstone hills run almost the entire length of the state. This region includes Oklahoma's second-largest city, Tulsa.

In the south, the plains eventually give way to the rolling Red River region. This area of the state, along the Texas border, was important to Oklahoma's early petroleum industry, and major oil fields are still found there. The Red River

Oklahoma has
77 counties.

Tulsa, one of the state's largest cities, is located on the Arkansas River.

region extends all the way to the state's southeastern corner, where it meets up with the Ouachitas. This fertile area is known for its rolling prairie and forests. The sandy soil is among the state's richest. Vegetables are a common sight growing in the fields.

The Red Bed Plains are found to the west of the sandstone hills. They form the largest land region in the state. Included in this region is the state capital, Oklahoma City. Like the sandstone hills, this area stretches from the Kansas border to southern Oklahoma's boundary with Texas. As the Red Beds gently slope upward to the west, a few forests give way to grasslands. The land supports some farming and livestock herding. The soil is made up of a combination of materials, mostly clay mixed with harder layers of sandstone and gypsum. The region is crossed by several streams, which flow from the High Plains located to the northwest.

The low-rising Arbuckle Mountains add to the variety of Central Oklahoma landforms. The Arbuckles cover about 1,000 square miles (2,600 sq km) in the south-central part of the state. They are an ancient mountain system. Granite found in Johnston County, just north of the Texas border, is about 1.4 billion years old. The portion of the Arbuckles in this area is the oldest exposed rock

Turner Falls, with a drop of 77 feet (23 m), is the largest waterfall in Oklahoma.

between the southern Appalachians to the east and the Rocky Mountains to the west.

The Arbuckles were once tall peaks. But many thousands of years of erosion have smoothed and flattened the range. They now rise from about 700 feet (215 m) above sea level in the east to 1,400 feet (425 m) in the west. The Chickasaw National Recreation Area, Turner Falls, Price Falls, and the Arbuckle Wilderness Park are some of the natural attractions found in this part of the state. The Arbuckles also contain commercially valuable minerals, such as iron ore, lead, zinc, limestone, and granite.

Western Oklahoma

Oklahoma's portion of the Great Plains is found in the west. This

Playa lakes in Western Oklahoma may be dry for much of the year but are filled with rainwater in the spring.

elevated region consists mostly of thick grasslands. It is also home to wheat fields and the grazing lands that fatten many of the state's livestock. This area is sometimes called the High Plains. The grasslands rise gently from about 2,000 feet (610 m) in the region's eastern edge to almost 5,000 feet (1,525 m) at the western end of the Panhandle. This portion of Oklahoma is but a small part of the immense grasslands that extend northward from central Texas all the way up into Canada. The flat surface of the High Plains is broken only by large streams and circular features often called sinks or playa lakes, which fill with water after spring rains but may be dry at other times of the year. These small bodies of water are scattered across the plains and help support the area's wildlife.

Like the rest of the state, Western Oklahoma offers its share of surprises. Sudden outcroppings of sandstone and gypsum, sharp ravines, and stark hills leave their mark on the northwest and the Panhandle. The southwest is also home to one of the state's most impressive mountain chains, the Wichitas. These granite peaks are about 525 million years old. They once towered 3,000 to 5,000 feet (915 to 1,525 m) above the plains but, as with the Arbuckles, millions of years of erosion have reduced their size.

Today, the Wichitas range from 400 to 1,100 feet (125 to 335 m), though some peaks reach above 2,400 feet (735 m). Mount Scott at 2,464 feet (751 m) is perhaps the best-known peak in the range. Its summit, or highest point, can be reached on foot or by car or bus. The view from Mount Scott reveals some of the state's most stunning scenery, including a great view of the region's many human-made lakes, or reservoirs. These lakes were created by damming the many streams that flow out of the range. The area has become a valuable source of granite, limestone, and sand and gravel. Smaller amounts of gold, silver, copper, lead, zinc, aluminum, and iron ores are found in the Wichitas.

The Gypsum Hills are another important part of Western Oklahoma. They lie west of

Bison and other grazing animals thrive in the grasslands of Western Oklahoma.

A roadway leads to the top of Mount Scott, from which visitors can enjoy spectacular views of the surrounding countryside.

the Red Bed Plains and eventually meet the High Plains in the northwestern portion of the state. These hills range in height from 150 to 200 feet (45 to 60 m). Each of the hills is capped with a layer of gypsum 15 to 20 feet (5 to 6 m) thick. The gypsum is mined to make plaster and other products. From a distance, the Gypsum Hills seem to sparkle in the sunlight. Because of that unique feature, they are sometimes called the Glass Hills.

At first glance, Western Oklahoma appears to be a dry, almost desertlike region. But the area receives enough rainfall to be blanketed with a variety of wildflowers and prairie grasses, such as little bluestem and hairy grama. Red cedars also dot the landscape.

Climate

Although Oklahoma is generally known for its warm, dry climate, state residents experience a wide range of weather. The northwest tends to be cooler and a bit drier than areas in the southeast. Winter months can easily see the temperature dropping below 0 degrees Fahrenheit (–18 degrees Celsius). North winds often descend on the Great Plains with their icy blasts.

In summer, the sun beats down on the treeless grasslands, and few things stir during the height of the midday heat. Temperatures can often rise well above 100 °F (38 °C). Hot, dry, and windy conditions can lead to prairie fires.

TORNADO ALLEY AND DIXIE ALLEY

Climate scientists classify Oklahoma as part of two separate tornado regions. The first region is Tornado Alley, which extends from Texas northward to South Dakota. This area gets most of its tornadoes in late spring. The second region is Dixie Alley, which ranges from Texas and Oklahoma across the Deep South. In this area, tornadoes typically occur in late fall.

Another weather-related disaster that can break the relative summer calm is a tornado. On average, the state is visited by more than fifty of these dangerous and damaging storms each year. In 2010, an especially heavy year, the state experienced more than one hundred tornadoes. May is typically the worst month for tornadoes in Oklahoma.

Precipitation, the amount of moisture the state receives, can vary greatly throughout the state. The southeast averages about 50 inches (127 centimeters) of precipitation per year. Conditions are very different in the Panhandle, which receives an average of 15 inches (38 cm) of precipitation annually. Snowstorms are rare in the southeast, dropping an annual average of only 2 inches (5 cm) on the region.

Tornadoes can cause severe damage to homes and other buildings.

Hot and dry weather can sometimes cause prairie fires on the Oklahoma plains.

People living in the Panhandle, though, have to shovel their way through up to 25 inches (64 cm) of snow per year.

Oklahoma Wildlife

Oklahoma's diverse terrain is home to a wide range of plants and animals. Oak, hickory, elm, pine, and ash are some of the trees that make up the woodlands of Eastern Oklahoma. White-tailed deer, raccoons, foxes, squirrels, and opossums make their homes in and among the trees.

As a prairie state, Oklahoma is also known for its wild grasses. These grasses help to feed the state's livestock and have colorful names such as bluestem, grama, wiregrass, and sandgrass. Grasses are not the only plants on the prairie. Sagebrush, mesquite, goldenrod, sunflowers, and black-eyed Susans are just a few of the other hearty plants that thrive on the plains. Black-tailed jackrabbits, pocket gophers, and kit foxes roam through the thick grass.

With so many reservoirs and natural lakes, the state is a sport-fishing paradise. Oklahoma is known as bass country, but other species, or types, of fish also are abundant. Sunfish, crappies, catfish, and carp gather near the shores or swim along the bottoms of the state's waterways.

STATE FISH

The sandbass, also known as the white bass or silver bass, is the official state fish. It is found in just about every major lake in Oklahoma. The record for the largest sandbass caught in the state is 5 pounds, 4 ounces (2.4 kilograms).

Many bird species inhabit the Sooner State. Often, large flocks blot the sky, or a single bird can be seen soaring—the only thing moving above the plains. Meadowlarks perch on fence posts, tilt back their heads, and fill the air with song. Blue jays, cardinals, doves, crows, and mockingbirds gather as well.

The Gypsum Hills are a great place to see the range of plants and animals the state has to offer. Bobcats and coyotes pad about the underbrush in search of a meal. Black-tailed prairie dogs keep a constant watch near their underground dens. They scurry down their holes at the first sign of danger. Armadillos, deer, and roadrunners are common sights as well. Collared lizards, western rattlesnakes, and tarantulas can be found in the shade, hiding from the hot rays of the midday sun.

Under many bridges and outcroppings in the Gypsum Hills, colonies of cliff swallows build their hanging nests out of mud. Fruit from the area's many red cedars attracts winged visitors from far away. During the winter, flocks of mountain bluebirds descend on the region, hundreds of miles from where they usually make their homes. They feed in the cedars, which also draw a number of birds that have headed south for the winter. Robins, cedar waxwings, and Townsend's solitaires can also be seen flitting among the trees.

Protecting the Environment

Oklahomans love their land and work hard to protect the plants and animals that live there. Conservation efforts require cooperation. Almost 95 percent of the state's land is privately owned. When there are problems, owners must agree to let wildlife officials step in and offer a solution. Too often, officials and groups take action only when a species is already endangered or threatened. Endangered species are plants and animals that are now so rare they may soon become extinct

Black-tailed prairie dogs stand about 12 inches (30 cm) tall and weigh about 1.5 pounds (0.7 kg).

(that is, completely die out). Threatened species are plants and animals that are likely to become endangered soon if nothing is done to preserve them.

Some concerned Oklahomans are working to prevent species from becoming threatened or endangered. They help ailing plant and animal communities recover and increase their numbers in the state before it is too late. The Partners for Fish and Wildlife Program links the federal government, the states, and private landowners in conservation activities. In 1990, Oklahoma began participating in this program, which works to restore land and improve animal populations on privately owned lands across the state.

At first, the program targeted wetlands. Later, wildlife officials focused on improving other areas where threatened and endangered plants and animals live. So far, more than 900 projects have been started, affecting practically every Oklahoma county. More than 300,000 acres (120,000 hectares) of wildlife habitat have been restored, including more than 22,000 acres (9,000 ha) of prairie wetlands. These valuable areas support migrating birds and a range of local species.

Conservation workers and concerned citizens know that it takes more than just projects to protect the environment. They believe education is key to ensuring the future of Oklahoma's wildlife. Under the Partners for Fish and Wildlife Program, more than 130 outdoor environmental classrooms have been set up or are being developed in Oklahoma. In these outdoor settings, students can learn about the natural world and what they can do to preserve it. Program officials expect to educate more than 2 million students in these special outdoor learning centers. Officials hope that these centers will improve students' understanding of how valuable their state's land, animals, and plants really are.

Plants & Animals

Wild Turkey

The wild turkey is Oklahoma's official state game bird. Two species make their homes in Oklahoma. The Rio Grande turkey is found in large numbers across the state, and the eastern wild turkey is located mostly in the state's southeastern and northeastern regions. The wild turkey was almost wiped out in Oklahoma by the early 1940s, but effective wildlife management has restored the turkey population.

Sandbass

Across the state, in natural lakes and reservoirs, "sandies" are a prize catch. Sandies travel in large schools, or groups. They eat other fish—mostly shad—and insects as well. Sandies usually live three or four years, but some live as long as ten years.

Armadillo

The bony, scaly shell of the nine-banded armadillo protects it from predators. Armadillos are good diggers and also good swimmers. They eat insects, grubs, and occasionally berries and birds' eggs. When female nine-banded armadillos reproduce, they give birth to four identical babies.

Prairie Rattlesnake

If you are hiking in the wilds of Oklahoma, keep alert for prairie rattlesnakes coiled beneath rocks. A prairie rattlesnake will attack if provoked, although its venom is rarely deadly to humans. It lives mainly in grasslands, but in winter it moves to dens in outcroppings and rocky ledges. It feeds on small rodents, birds that nest on the ground, and sometimes other snakes.

Red Bat

This nighttime flyer is the only species of bat in North America in which the female and male are different colors. The females tend to be yellow-brown, while the males can be a bright shade of orange. Red bats roost in trees, and they can eat more than a thousand insects per hour.

Indian Blanket

The Indian blanket is Oklahoma's state wildflower. It usually blooms from June to August and reaches from 1 to 3 feet (0.3 to 0.9 m) in height. The flower is red in the center with yellow on the tips. This resilient flower thrives in both extreme heat and drought conditions.

From the Beginning

Humans have been living in Oklahoma for more than 12,000 years. At a site near Anadarko, archaeologists—scientists who study the past—found several spear points and the bones of a mammoth (a large mammal that is now extinct). They have connected these artifacts with a group of people known as the Clovis culture. This ancient group most likely wandered into the region following herds of animals. The plains proved to be an ideal place to search for food. Many prehistoric creatures came to the grasslands to graze and mate. Giant mammoths, musk-oxen, ground sloths, elk, reindeer, bears, and an early version of the horse all made the plains their home.

Eventually these early people of the Clovis culture shifted their focus to one main food source—the bison. Small groups of people would follow the wandering herds for part or most of the year. They also gathered plants, eating whatever they could find. These hunter-gatherers would build temporary shelters, live in them for a brief time, and then move on.

About 2,500 years ago, another shift occurred. People settled into a more stable lifestyle. Farming, mostly of corn and beans, became important.

From 500 to 1300 CE, a group known as the Mound Builders lived in what would become Le Flore County, just west of the Arkansas-Oklahoma border. They built huge earthen mounds to honor their dead. Artifacts found in these burial mounds show that the Mound Builders made artwork and many useful objects by

This prehistoric shell carving, an ornament that was worn around the neck, was found at the Spiro Mounds archaeological site in Eastern Oklahoma.

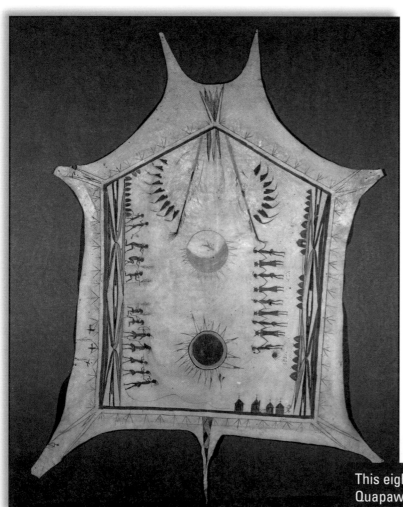
hand. They also had a complex economy that involved a large trading network. It stretched from the Great Lakes to the Pacific coast.

By the time Europeans arrived in the region in the sixteenth century, members of the Caddo Nation were living in what is now southeastern Oklahoma. The Quapaw settled in present-day northeastern Oklahoma, where they lived as farmers and hunter-gatherers. The Wichita adopted a similar lifestyle. They built grass houses often along rivers and streams in the southern and eastern parts of the area. Later arrivals in the northeast, the Osage, mostly farmed. But their hunting parties made annual bison hunts on the plains to the west. Groups of Cheyenne, Arapaho, Comanche, and Plains Apache Indians would also enter what is now Western Oklahoma, following the bison herds. The Kiowa and Pawnee were other major Indian nations in the region, adding to the great variety of tribes living on the plains.

This eighteenth-century map showing Quapaw villages was painted on bison skin.

Europeans Arrive

The first European to enter present-day Oklahoma was most likely Francisco Vásquez de Coronado. He crossed the region in 1541, leading an expedition that started in present-day New Mexico. Hernando de Soto, another Spanish explorer, may have passed through what is now Eastern Oklahoma as well. They were both in search of gold and, finding none, soon moved on.

In 1601, Juan de Oñate also traveled through the western portion of the present-day state in search of gold. His group reached the site of today's city of Wichita, Kansas, then turned around and headed back to the Southwest. Oñate was followed by additional Spanish explorers and by French traders from Louisiana looking for new markets for their goods. A seventeenth-century French explorer, René-Robert Cavelier, sieur de La Salle, claimed the area for France on his journey down the Mississippi River valley. But the Spanish and French newcomers found little to make them stay in the region. The first European trading post was most likely established at Salina in the early 1800s.

At the beginning of the nineteenth century, France held present-day Oklahoma as part of the Louisiana Territory. In 1803, the U.S. government paid $15 million to buy the entire territory from France. This land sale, known as the Louisiana Purchase, brought what is now Oklahoma under U.S. government control.

In the sixteenth century, Hernando de Soto and other Spanish explorers probably passed through present-day Oklahoma as they searched for gold in the region.

Following the Louisiana Purchase, some important white settlements sprang up, including Miller Court House, located in today's McCurtain County, and Three Forks in the northeast. But beyond the occasional trader, explorer, or curious traveler, most of the region stayed in the hands of American Indians. Because of the area's remote location, the Indians' contacts with whites developed slowly. As the Wichita and other Indian nations began trading with outsiders, the introduction of cloth, cookware, guns, and other items began to transform the Indian way of life.

The Trail of Tears

In the 1830s and 1840s, the U.S. government took actions against American Indians in the eastern United States that would affect the Oklahoma region for decades to come. The government began a campaign to remove and relocate certain American Indian groups from the southeastern states to land west of the Mississippi River. The Cherokee, Choctaw, Chickasaw, Creek, and Seminole peoples—known as the Five Civilized Tribes—had made parts of Georgia, Florida, and Alabama their home for hundreds of years. Now they were forced to leave their homeland behind and enter the strange new landscape of the Great Plains. To prepare for the large number of newcomers, federal officials built Fort Towson, Fort Gibson, and other facilities in what is now Oklahoma.

Few of the Indians came of their own free will. In 1838–1839, thousands of Cherokee were moved to the unclaimed "no-man's-land" of the southern plains. Much of the journey was made in harsh winter weather, and there were shortages of food and other supplies. About 4,000 Cherokee died while making this hard journey, now known as the Trail of Tears. The survivors eventually settled on the hills and plains of present-day Eastern Oklahoma. There, they set about the hard work of rebuilding their communities and their lives. Forced migrations of Indian groups continued in the 1840s.

All of what is now Oklahoma, except for the Panhandle (which in 1836 was claimed by the newly independent Texas Republic), was set aside by the U.S. government for American Indians. The area became known as Indian Territory or Indian Country. Over time, the relocated groups settled into their new homeland, where they organized their own new nations. They built homes and schools and established courts and legislatures, or groups that set up tribal laws. The Cherokee and Choctaw grew cotton, while the Creek and Chickasaw mostly herded livestock

In 1838–1839, as many as 15,000 Cherokee were forced to relocate from the southeastern United States to present-day Oklahoma, in the journey that became known as the Trail of Tears.

MAKING A CHEROKEE BEAR CLAW NECKLACE

The American Indians who were moved into Oklahoma's Indian Territory were proud of the traditional crafts they brought from their ancestral lands. Jewelry was one of the treasured art forms. By following these instructions, you can make an imitation of a bear claw necklace worn by members of the Cherokee Nation.

WHAT YOU NEED

Several sheets of newspaper

1 pound (0.45 kg) of self-hardening clay (found at craft stores)

Ruler

Butter knife

Large nail or knitting needle

Acrylic paints—dark brown, white, and any other colors

Paintbrushes

2 feet (0.6 m) of twine, shoelaces, or rawhide lacing

Spread the newspaper over your work surface, because working with the clay can be messy. Knead the clay for a few minutes to soften it. Pull off a small piece of clay, and roll it into a bear claw shape, about $1\frac{1}{2}$ inches (3.8 cm) long and no more than $\frac{1}{4}$ inch (0.6 cm) thick. Use the ruler to measure the size. You can use the knife to help shape the clay, but be careful since the knife can be sharp. (You can ask an adult for help cutting and shaping the clay.) Make four more claws, all about the same size. For all five claws, have an adult help you use the nail or knitting needle to make a hole through the thickest part of each claw. Set aside the claws while you make the clay beads.

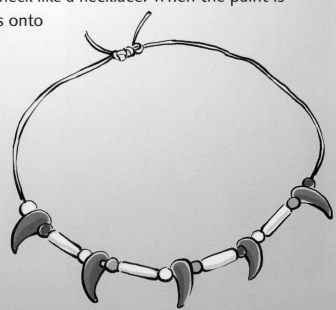

Break off four small pieces of clay. With your fingers, roll them out to make long bone beads about $^1/_2$ inch (1.3 cm) thick and $^3/_4$ inch (1.9 cm) long. Carefully push the nail or knitting needle through each.

Break off ten small pieces of clay and roll them into small round beads. Carefully push the nail or knitting needle through each of these beads.

Put all the claws and beads in a flat, dry place, and let them harden. This should take about one to two days.

Once the clay pieces are dry, get ready to paint them. Spread more newspaper on your work surface. Using the acrylic paints, color the bear claws dark brown and color the long bone beads white. You can use any other colors for the small round beads.

While the paint is drying, take the twine or lacing and cut a piece long enough to drape around your neck like a necklace. When the paint is dry, string the claws and beads onto the twine or lacing. Alternate claws, bone beads, and round beads in whatever pattern you like. Tie the ends of the twine together—use a double knot to make sure the necklace stays tied. You can wear your necklace or show it to your friends and family.

The Civil War and Beyond

From 1861 to 1865, the North and South fought against each other in the Civil War. During this war, no major battles took place in Oklahoma, although several skirmishes occurred there. Loyalties in the region were divided. Having come from the South, some of the American Indians had African-American slaves. When it came time to choose sides, a majority of the Indians supported the South, which was also called the Confederacy. At first, the Cherokee were reluctant to favor either the Union (the North) or the Confederacy. But representatives from the Confederate states of Texas and Arkansas met with them, urging them to support the South. Eventually the Cherokee Nation agreed to side with the Confederacy.

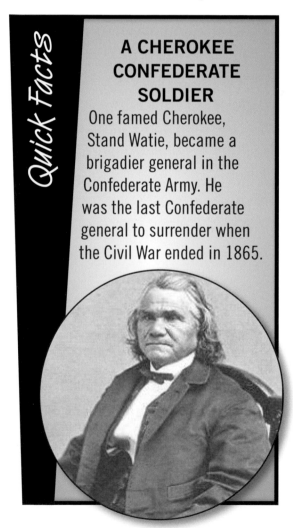

Quick Facts

A CHEROKEE CONFEDERATE SOLDIER
One famed Cherokee, Stand Watie, became a brigadier general in the Confederate Army. He was the last Confederate general to surrender when the Civil War ended in 1865.

When the Union won the Civil War, Oklahoma's Indian nations were punished for having supported the losing side. The western part of Indian Territory, which had originally been granted to the Five Civilized Tribes, was taken away from them and divided among other Indian groups. Peoria, Ottawa, Wyandot, and Miami Indians began farming on reservations established there. Cheyenne, Kiowa, Comanche, and Arapaho Indians, who were used to the wide-open spaces of the plains, had more difficulty adjusting to the often cramped living conditions on the reservations.

With the Kiowa, Comanche, Cheyenne, and Arapaho, the United States signed the Little Arkansas Treaties in 1865. The American Indian nations agreed to remain peaceful and to limit the size of their hunting ranges. In exchange, the U.S. government vowed to protect and support the Indian nations. The treaties promised the Indians the power to own and govern their new homelands. But the U.S government had little concern for honoring these rights. Two years later, in a group of agreements known as the Treaty of Medicine Lodge Creek, the Indian lands were greatly reduced.

After the Civil War, the flow of white settlers onto the southern plains increased. Soon the newcomers pushed up against the borders of American Indian land. The unclaimed expanses of free land surrounding Indian Territory were soon taken. Non-Indian people seeking a new and better life along the American frontier flooded into the area. To make matters worse, hunters—mostly from the eastern United States— killed tens of thousands of bison, taking an important source of food away from the Indians in the region.

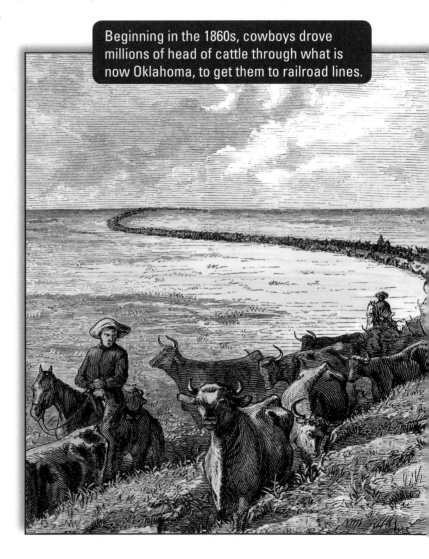

Beginning in the 1860s, cowboys drove millions of head of cattle through what is now Oklahoma, to get them to railroad lines.

The Changing Plains

With the arrival of so many new people, the region's economy began to expand. The area became a crossroads for the many cattle herds being moved from the ranches of Texas to railroad lines in Kansas. Ranchers drove their herds across what is now Oklahoma, pausing to fatten the valuable animals on the grasses of the plains. Some cattlemen paid the American Indians for the right to have their herds graze on Indian-held lands. Most did not.

Soon, several well-traveled cattle trails crossed the region. The Chisholm Trail became the best known, but the Western, East Shawnee, and West Shawnee trails were also heavily used. Between 1866 and 1885, more than 6 million head of Texas longhorn cattle crossed American Indian lands. Slowly, ranchers became convinced of the value of owning what was once considered bleak and useless land. When the railroad came to Oklahoma in the early 1870s, the region became even more valuable in the eyes of ranchers and other settlers.

People eager to obtain land in Oklahoma in 1889 quickly set up tent cities and staked their claims when the U.S. government opened a large area to new settlers.

Boomers and Sooners

By the late 1800s, many settlers were eager to claim Indian lands for themselves. Called Boomers, these settlers were led by William L. Couch, Charles C. Carpenter, and David L. Payne. They put pressure on the U.S. government to open Indian lands for settlement by others.

Eventually, the government yielded. From the Creek and the Seminole, it bought more than 3 million acres (1.2 million ha). This parcel was added to lands taken from other Indian nations. A large part of what is now Central Oklahoma was then declared open for settlement in 1889. On April 22, eager land-grabbers lined up along the border, awaiting the signal to head into the so-called Unassigned Lands. At noon, the Unassigned Lands were officially opened. The signal brought a mad dash as settlers raced into the unclaimed area. They were in search of a prime stretch of countryside to call their own. Those who had sneaked into the territory illegally, before the official signal, were known as Sooners. Oklahoma residents have been nicknamed Sooners ever since.

Indian Territory and Oklahoma Territory

The Oklahoma region had been known since the 1830s as Indian Territory or Indian Country. This changed on May 2, 1890, when the region was divided into two parts. One was still called Indian Territory, while the other was named the Oklahoma Territory. Indian Territory included the remaining lands of the Five Civilized Tribes plus the limited holdings

> **EXPANDING THE RAILS**
> *Quick Facts*
>
> In 1880, the rail network in the Oklahoma region totaled only 289 miles (465 km). By 1920, Oklahoma had 6,572 miles (10,577 km) of rail lines.

> **A FAST-GROWING CITY**
> *Quick Facts*
>
> On the morning of April 22, 1889, what is now Oklahoma City was nothing more than a stretch of barren prairie. By nightfall, more than 10,000 people had descended on the area. Today, Oklahoma City is home to about 580,000 people.

of other tribes. The Oklahoma Territory included the former Unassigned Lands, along with the Panhandle (then known as No Man's Land), which had earlier belonged to Texas. George Washington Steele was named the Oklahoma Territory's first governor.

The largest land rush in the history of the Oklahoma Territory took place on September 16, 1893. That was the day a huge tract of land in the north-central part of the region was first opened to non-Indian settlers. Most of this land consisted of what was known as the Cherokee Outlet, an area the Indians had essentially been forced to sell to the U.S. government at a very low price. When this land became available to settlers, more than 50,000 people descended on the region. Many of the newcomers, who were known as homesteaders, were not prepared for the hard life they faced on the open plains. All they saw was free land and not the challenges and responsibilities that came with it. For every farm or ranch that succeeded, many others failed.

Many homesteaders abandoned their plots of land. Wealthy landowners, often called land barons, then bought up these abandoned homesteads. By the late 1890s, many settlers who arrived in the region found there was only land to rent, not own. By 1900, 40 percent of Oklahoma's farmers were tenant farmers. These tenant farmers rented the land from the owner and paid the landowner a portion of their crops in exchange. This arrangement between tenant farmers and landowners was known as sharecropping.

The Path to Statehood

In 1893 a special group called the Dawes Commission was set up to divide some of the remaining American Indian lands into smaller pieces. These parcels of land in Indian Territory were to go to Indian families or individuals. U.S. officials saw the program as a way of reducing what little control some Indian nations still had over their tracts of land. Agents helped the Indians set up towns and prepare to become American citizens.

Slowly, Indian Territory became a mixture of white settlers and Indians who owned their own private plots of land. The population grew. By 1905, many

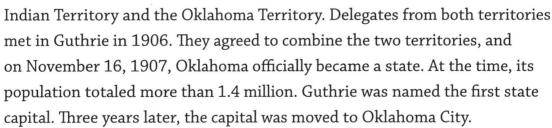

Oil gushes from an Oklahoma well in the early 1900s. The discovery of major oil deposits brought new wealth to the state by the beginning of the twentieth century.

people in Indian Territory believed it was ready for statehood. The Five Civilized Tribes called a constitutional convention at Muskogee. White settlers were invited to take part as well. They outnumbered the Indians by five to one. At the end of the convention, they all agreed to create the state of Sequoyah. The action was then approved by a majority of voters in Indian Territory.

The U.S. Congress refused to consider the Sequoyah plan. Instead, federal officials wanted to create one state called Oklahoma out of both Indian Territory and the Oklahoma Territory. Delegates from both territories met in Guthrie in 1906. They agreed to combine the two territories, and on November 16, 1907, Oklahoma officially became a state. At the time, its population totaled more than 1.4 million. Guthrie was named the first state capital. Three years later, the capital was moved to Oklahoma City.

In the first decade of the 1900s, the state's economy boomed, largely because of a growing oil industry. After early oil finds at Chelsea in 1889 and Bartlesville in 1897, the opening of the Red Fork–Tulsa oil field in 1901 made Tulsa the center of Oklahoma's oil business. Cattle ranching, though on the decline, remained a major source of the state's income. At the same time, crops such as corn, wheat, and cotton added to Oklahoma's wealth. But farming was still a hard life for many of Oklahoma's residents.

Injured people arrested after racial violence in Tulsa in 1921 are taken by truck to a hospital to receive medical attention.

War and Racial Violence

In 1917, the United States entered World War I (1914–1918). About 91,000 Oklahomans served in the military during the conflict. More than 1,000 troops from Oklahoma were killed in action, and about 4,500 were wounded.

During wartime, demand increased for crops and food products, which Oklahoma's farmers helped to supply. But after this short period of prosperity, the state's fortunes took a turn for the worse. Farm prices dropped, making it hard for farmers to earn a living. The Ku Klux Klan (KKK), a secret organization that supported violence against African Americans and other minorities, gained in popularity across the state. The Klan's influence spread to city and county governments, in which some KKK members held important positions. In 1921, in one of Tulsa's darkest moments, angry white mobs threatened to kill an African-American man falsely accused of hurting a white woman. When residents of the African-American neighborhood of Greenwood resisted, a gun battle erupted, and many buildings were set ablaze. As many as 300 African Americans were killed, and most of the Greenwood neighborhood was destroyed.

Dust Bowl Days

When farm prices fell after World War I, farmers tried to plant more crops to make up for their losses, but this only made matters worse. The overworked soil yielded poorer harvests. At the same time, overgrazing by the state's many cattle removed much of the grass from Oklahoma's rangelands. This further weakened the quality of Oklahoma's soil.

By the beginning of the 1930s, the nation was in the grips of the Great Depression. During this period of economic hardship, millions of Americans could not find jobs, and families struggled to survive. Banks closed, taking people's life savings with them. In Oklahoma, extremely hot summers and lack of rainfall made matters worse. Crops withered and died in the fields. Drought spread across the plains. High winds raised huge clouds of dust. At times, the clouds were so large and thick they seemed to blot out the daylight. The American prairie became known as the Dust Bowl. Oklahoma was at the heart of it.

In Their Own Words

I've seen the wind so high that it blowed my fences down,

Buried my tractor six feet underground.

Well, it turned my farm into a pile of sand,

Yes, it turned my farm into a pile of sand, . . .

These dusty blues are the dustiest ones I know,

Buried head over heels in the black old dust,

I had to pack up and go.

—folksinger Woody Guthrie, "Dust Bowl Blues"

Dust storms, such as this one in Cimarron County in 1936, blew away soil from many Oklahoma farms.

Completed in the 1950s, the Fort Gibson Dam produces electricity and created a lake behind it that attracts boaters, fishers, and other lovers of the outdoors.

In the years after World War II, the manufacturing of aircraft parts became an important industry in Oklahoma.

Many of the state's farmers, ranchers, and other workers decided to leave. Okies, as they were called, moved west in the hope of leaving the hard times behind them. As a result, the state lost more than 300,000 residents. But times were tough everywhere.

Eventually the drought ended. People learned a harsh lesson from the Dust Bowl years and began to use the land more wisely. Aid from the federal government helped the state's economy to recover. Between 1941 and 1945, while the United States was directly involved in World War II, demand grew for the state's two main products, crops and oil. Military bases, built outside of Enid and Oklahoma City, also created much-needed jobs.

Oklahoma After World War II

The second half of the twentieth century brought further changes. Dams and irrigation projects improved farmlands, provided electric power, and created lakes for recreation. Strong governors led the way in improving education, reforming

New industries in Oklahoma in recent years include wind farms that use the high winds of the open plains to produce electricity.

prisons, and strengthening the ways the state handled its finances. New industries and construction projects boosted the state's economy in the 1960s. Electronics plants were built in Oklahoma City. The state capital also became the home of a major center for the Federal Aviation Administration (FAA). This important FAA facility trained airport workers and conducted research into airplane safety. Farther east, Tulsa became the site of factories making parts for airplanes and spacecraft. Today, more than 14,000 people in the Tulsa area have jobs in the aerospace industry.

In the 1970s, Oklahoma's abundance of open land, fuel, water, and electric power continued to attract companies to the state. In 1971, the Oklahoma portion of the Arkansas River Navigation System opened. This made it easier for products from Muskogee and Tulsa to reach major U.S. cities and ports, linking Oklahoma with the growing global economy. During this decade, a dramatic rise in oil prices brought another boost to the state's income. But in the 1980s, when oil prices declined, the state's economy experienced a steep drop. Oil wells across the state were shut down.

During the 1990s, state leaders looked for ways to broaden the state's sources of income. New businesses were lured to the state, requiring workers trained in an ever wider variety of skills. Tourism, technology, and educational and health services took on increased importance.

The Oklahoma City Bombing and After

On April 19, 1995, another dark chapter was added to the state's history. On an otherwise quiet morning in Oklahoma City, a truck filled with explosives, driven by a man named Timothy McVeigh, blew up in front of the Alfred P. Murrah Federal Building. The bombing killed 168 Oklahomans, including 19 young children in a child-care center on the building's first floor. More than 500 other people were injured. McVeigh escaped but was later arrested. He was convicted in 1997 of murder and other crimes, and he was put to death four years later.

After the Oklahoma City bombing, rescue workers cut through the wreckage of the Murrah Building looking for survivors of the blast.

The Oklahoma City National Memorial includes a "Field of Empty Chairs"—168 chairs in all—honoring the memory of the victims of the 1995 Oklahoma City bombing.

A memorial, at the site where the bombed building once stood, has attracted millions of visitors since it opened in 2000. It ensures that people will never forget those who lost their lives because of McVeigh's terrorist act.

In recent years, the state has benefited from large increases in prices for oil and natural gas. Oklahoma has become one of the nation's leading natural gas producers, supplying about 8 percent of annual U.S. output. When the nation's economy slowed down beginning in late 2007, Oklahoma fared better than many other states. Reversing a pattern set decades earlier, Oklahoma even began attracting people and jobs from California and other western states.

Important Dates

★ **10,000** BCE People of the Clovis culture hunt mammoths and other large mammals.

★ **500** CE People of the Mound Builders culture settle in present-day Eastern Oklahoma.

★ **1541** Francisco Vásquez de Coronado becomes the first European to enter present-day Oklahoma.

★ **1682** Land including what is now Oklahoma is claimed for France by the explorer La Salle.

★ **1803** In the Louisiana Purchase, the United States buys from France a huge area of land that includes what is now Oklahoma.

★ **1819** All of the present-day state, except for the Panhandle, becomes part of the new Arkansas Territory.

★ **1830s–1842** The Five Civilized Tribes are relocated to what becomes known as Indian Territory.

★ **1865–1867** Punished for siding with the Confederacy during the Civil War, the Five Civilized Tribes lose much of their land.

★ **1872** The first railway line is laid across the region.

★ **1889** Oklahoma's Unassigned Lands are opened to white settlement.

★ **1890** The Oklahoma region is reorganized as two territories—the Oklahoma Territory and Indian Territory.

★ **1907** Oklahoma, including both territories, becomes the forty-sixth state.

★ **1921** Racial violence in Tulsa claims up to 300 African-American lives.

★ **1930s** Severe drought and high winds turn Oklahoma's dried-out soil into the Dust Bowl. Hundreds of thousands of people leave the state in search of opportunity elsewhere.

★ **1995** A terrorist's truck bomb destroys the Alfred P. Murrah Federal Building in Oklahoma City, killing 168 people.

★ **2007** Oklahoma celebrates 100 years of statehood.

★ **2011** An earthquake measuring 5.6 on the Richter scale is the strongest in Oklahoma's recorded history.

3
The People

When Oklahoma became the forty-sixth state in 1907, its residents were already a blend of many cultures and traditions. Oklahomans included cotton farmers from the South, wheat farmers from the Midwest, and cattle ranchers from the West. American Indians, African Americans, and people of European descent were all part of the population. While many people had come to farm the land, by the twentieth century, others were drawn by the rise of the petroleum industry.

When coal fields near McAlester were opened in the late 1800s, European immigrants flooded into the region. Newcomers from Wales, Ireland, Poland, Russia, Italy, France, and Lithuania made the McAlester area one of the most diverse in the territory.

Other groups created their own towns on the plains. German Mennonites who had earlier immigrated to Russia brought sacks of Crimean hard wheat to their new American homes. They started farming communities named Corn, Colony, and Bessie in Western Oklahoma. Czech immigrants, mostly arriving from other parts of the Midwest, settled in towns such as Prague, Yukon, and Mishak. Slaves freed by the American Indians, as well as new arrivals from the South, built a chain of mostly African-American towns across the plains. Boley, Red Bird, Rentiesville, and Langston are just a few of the communities that still exist to this day.

Indians in Oklahoma preserve their traditions at events such as the American Indian Exposition in Anadarko.

Traditional dances are part of the annual Czech Festival in Yukon, a town that attracted many immigrants of Czech heritage to Oklahoma.

In recent years, new groups have arrived. They are adding to the changing face of Oklahoma. No matter how diverse the newcomers may be, most of them are drawn to the state for similar reasons. Community pride, good schools, and a slower pace of life help make the Sooner State a great place to live.

Hispanic Americans and Asian Americans

Oklahoma's Hispanic population more than tripled between 1990 and 2010, and Hispanic Americans now make up about 9 percent of the state's population. Most Hispanics in Oklahoma are of Mexican origin. Many others are of Puerto Rican or Cuban heritage. The growth of the Hispanic population has been concentrated in and around the state's major cities. Hispanics make up about 17 percent of the population in Oklahoma City and 14 percent in Tulsa. Oklahoma City, with about 580,000 people, is the largest city in the state, and Tulsa, with about 390,000 people, is the second largest. Hispanic Americans in Oklahoma work in many careers and run many types of businesses. In Tulsa's Little Mexico neighborhood, restaurants and food stores offer people of all cultures a taste of Mexican cooking and traditional foods.

Although they still account for less than 2 percent of the state's total population, Asian Americans represent one of Oklahoma's fastest-growing minority groups. Growth in the hog farming and processing industries has helped to attract some of the newcomers, who include thousands of people of Vietnamese heritage. After the Vietnam War ended in the mid-1970s, a large number of Vietnamese families came to the United States. But moving to the United States from Vietnam was expensive, and often relatives had to be left behind. Beginning in the late 1970s, Oklahoma welcomed a new wave of Vietnamese immigrants, reuniting families that had been divided during the first wave of immigration.

Youngsters look into the mouth of a dragon at a Vietnamese children's festival in Oklahoma City.

Famous Oklahomans

Will Rogers: Cowboy, Actor, and Humorist

Rogers, who was part Cherokee, was born on a ranch in Oologah, Indian Territory, in 1879. Skilled with a lasso, he dropped out of high school to become a cowboy. He soon found he could use his roping skills to entertain audiences as well as lasso steers. In the 1920s and early 1930s, he was one of the nation's most popular movie stars, storytellers, authors, and political humorists. Millions of Americans were saddened when Rogers died in a plane crash in Alaska in 1935.

Ralph Ellison: Writer

Born in Oklahoma City in 1914, Ellison briefly attended Alabama's Tuskegee Institute before moving to New York City to study sculpture. Soon, writing became his passion. The first African American to win the National Book Award, he published his only completed novel, *Invisible Man*, in 1952. The story of an African-American man who is losing his identity in a racist world, it is considered by many to be one of the best American novels of the twentieth century. Ellison died in 1994.

Maria Tallchief: Ballerina

Born in 1925 in Fairfax to Scottish-Irish and American Indian parents, Tallchief studied music and dance in California. She married choreographer George Balanchine in 1946, and when he founded the New York City Ballet, he chose Tallchief as a prima ballerina. Together they set the tone for American dance for two decades. She was an international star when she ended her performing career in 1966, although she remained active as a dance teacher and company director. Tallchief died in 2013.

Mickey Mantle: Baseball Player

Born in Spavinaw in 1931, this switch-hitting center fielder starred for 18 years with the New York Yankees. During his Yankee career, he led the American League in home runs four times, won three regular-season Most Valuable Player awards, and helped lead his team to seven World Series championships. Mantle was elected to the Baseball Hall of Fame in 1974. He died in Texas in 1995.

Shannon Lucid: Astronaut

Lucid was born in China in 1943 but grew up in Bethany. After receiving a Ph.D. in biochemistry from the University of Oklahoma, she became one of the first six women chosen by NASA to be an astronaut. She flew on five separate missions, for a total of 223 days in space. During her 1996 mission aboard the *Mir* space station, she conducted a variety of experiments, including growing wheat while in orbit. "It reminded me of Oklahoma," she said. Lucid retired from NASA in early 2012.

Carrie Underwood: Country Singer, Songwriter

Underwood was born in Muskogee in 1983 and grew up in Checotah. Her singing talent was recognized early, but her big break did not come until 2005, when she earned top honors on television's *American Idol*. Her first album, *Some Hearts*, earned Underwood a Grammy Award as Best New Artist in 2007. She remains one of country music's biggest stars, winning Entertainer of the Year awards in 2009 and 2010 from the Academy of Country Music. Underwood released her fourth album, *Blown Away*, in 2012.

About half of Oklahoma's African Americans are children or young adults under the age of 30.

African Americans

The 2010 Census counted more than 277,000 African Americans in Oklahoma. Most of the first black Oklahomans were slaves owned by members of the Five Civilized Tribes. When the Indians were forced west along the Trail of Tears, their slaves came with them. In parts of Oklahoma before the Civil War, some Indians were able to reestablish the plantation system they had known in the South. One Choctaw plantation totaled more than 5,000 acres (2,025 ha) and contained 500 slaves.

Later, African Americans came to the region as farmers, cowboys, and businesspeople. During the Civil War, escaped slaves and people of mixed race, usually of both black and American Indian heritage, played key roles in the Union's success. One historically important event was the Battle of Honey Springs, fought on July 17, 1863, outside present-day Muskogee. The battle, which was won by the Union, marked the first time regiments of whites, blacks, and American Indians fought on the same field. The First Kansas Colored Volunteer Infantry Regiment, as well as American Indian regiments, joined white Union troops to win the day. In his official report, Major General James G. Blunt wrote that the black troops had been the deciding factor in the Union's victory.

After the Civil War, Congress created the all-black Ninth and Tenth Cavalries. Made up mostly of veterans of the war, they were stationed in the Oklahoma region at Forts Gibson and Sill. These troops, known as buffalo soldiers, performed many roles on the frontier. They helped build new forts, fought the many bandits hiding out in the territory, and chased down cattle thieves. They also patrolled Indian reservations and helped move Sooners off land they had illegally seized.

From 1865 to 1920, African Americans in Oklahoma created over fifty all-black towns, more than in all other states combined. Some of these towns lasted for only a brief period. Others still exist today. For people escaping the shadow of slavery, Oklahoma was seen as a kind of paradise. African Americans could vote, study, and work with greater ease and freedom than in most other states. Black Oklahomans were also encouraged to start businesses, which they did in great numbers. Before the Tulsa riot of 1921 devastated the community, the mostly black section of town called Greenwood was also known as the Black Wall Street. Developed by a rich landowner named O. W. Gurley, Greenwood's thirty-five blocks were home to more than 11,000 residents, some of whom were prosperous business owners and millionaires. After the riot, black Oklahomans rebuilt Greenwood, and by the early 1940s, the district was home to more than 240 businesses that were owned or operated by African Americans.

In cities and towns, on the plains and the oil fields, black Oklahomans have made their lasting mark on the Sooner State. Today, Oklahoma's black

> # In Their Own Words
>
> *[The First Kansas Colored Volunteer Infantry Regiment] fought like veterans, and preserved their line unbroken throughout the engagement. Their coolness and bravery I have never seen surpassed; they were in the hottest of the fight, and opposed to Texas troops twice their number, whom they completely routed. One Texas regiment ... that fought against them went into the fight with 300 men and came out with only 60.*
>
> —Major General James G. Blunt

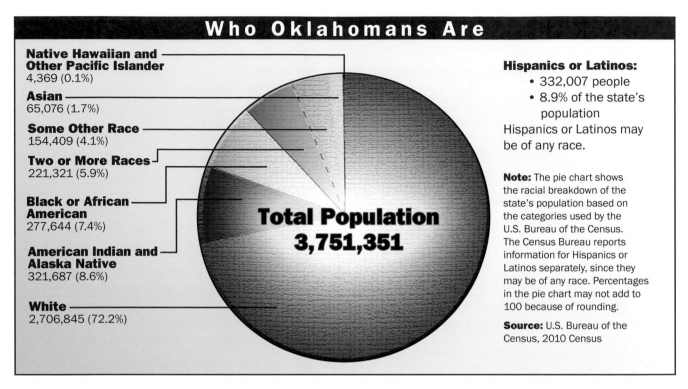

Who Oklahomans Are

Native Hawaiian and Other Pacific Islander
4,369 (0.1%)

Asian
65,076 (1.7%)

Some Other Race
154,409 (4.1%)

Two or More Races
221,321 (5.9%)

Black or African American
277,644 (7.4%)

American Indian and Alaska Native
321,687 (8.6%)

White
2,706,845 (72.2%)

Total Population 3,751,351

Hispanics or Latinos:
- 332,007 people
- 8.9% of the state's population

Hispanics or Latinos may be of any race.

Note: The pie chart shows the racial breakdown of the state's population based on the categories used by the U.S. Bureau of the Census. The Census Bureau reports information for Hispanics or Latinos separately, since they may be of any race. Percentages in the pie chart may not add to 100 because of rounding.

Source: U.S. Bureau of the Census, 2010 Census

community is as strong as ever. Reunions, rodeos, and Juneteenth celebrations—which mark the freeing of many slaves—are just some of the ways Oklahoma's African Americans celebrate their heritage.

Oklahoma Indians

More than 10 percent of all the American Indians now living in the United States make their homes in Oklahoma. The state government recognizes nearly forty Indian nations located within the state. Most Oklahoma Indians live in and around Tulsa and Oklahoma City. But many still live on reservations and in small communities throughout the state.

Oklahoma's Indians have made many efforts to develop local businesses and to keep Indian culture and traditions alive. In recent years, the leaders of Indian nations have encouraged their members to take a more active role in Oklahoma politics and government. The first steps are registering to vote and being counted in the census. These actions are designed to impress on state officials the voting strength and economic power of the state's Indian communities.

CENTENNIAL CELEBRATIONS

In 2007, Oklahomans marked the centennial, or one-hundredth anniversary, of statehood with a year-long series of celebrations, historical reenactments, and other events. In Guthrie, where delegates had met a century earlier to write Oklahoma's constitution, a number of dramatizations were staged showing highlights of the constitutional convention. Many of the reenactors were high school students. On October 14, downtown Oklahoma City hosted the Oklahoma Centennial Parade. About 175,000 people turned out to enjoy the parade's colorful floats, balloons, marching bands, and other performers. The following month, on November 16—the date of Oklahoma's admission to the Union—the Centennial Spectacular was staged at Oklahoma City's Ford Center (since renamed Chesapeake Energy Arena). The televised event featured performances by country music stars and other entertainers born in the state, including Carrie Underwood, Vince Gill, and Reba McEntire. Almost one-third of all Oklahomans watched the Centennial Spectacular broadcast.

Using a jet pack, stunt performer Dan Schlund, known as the Rocketman, lands during the finale of the Oklahoma Centennial Parade.

Calendar of Events

★ **Mangum Rattlesnake Derby**

Each April, participants in the annual Mangum Rattlesnake Derby compete to find the longest snake. Visitors who prefer tamer pastimes can enjoy a live snake show, snack on fried rattlesnake, or have a photo taken with a genuine live rattler. Rides, games, and square dancing add to the fun.

★ **Chuck Wagon Gathering and Children's Cowboy Festival**

At this Oklahoma City festival that kicks off in May, kids of all ages can try their hand at cowboy and frontier life through activities such as learning how to make rope, designing bandanas, and weaving. Wagon rides and a Shetland pony carousel add to the fun, as visitors to the National Cowboy and Western Heritage Museum enjoy an uproarious Old West show. There are also authentic foods prepared by chuck wagon crews.

★ **Red Earth Native American Cultural Festival**

Each June, Oklahoma City plays host to the largest American Indian visual and performing arts event of its kind. The festival features works by more than 1,200 Indian artists and dancers. Events include drum groups, dance competitions, and a grand parade in which more than 100 Indian nations are represented.

★ **American Heritage Music Festival**

Cloggers and fiddlers come to Grove each June to compete for cash prizes and the right to claim the title of grand champion. This weekend full of dancing and music is capped off by special performances each evening.

★ Woody Guthrie Folk Festival

This annual event, also known as WoodyFest, kicks off each July in Okemah, the performer's hometown. It was started to promote Guthrie's music and to honor his legacy. Folk, alternative, and acoustic performers provide the entertainment.

★ Arbuckle Mountain Bluegrass Festival

Head to Wynnewood for food, fun, and bluegrass music. Festivalgoers are treated to some of the best bluegrass musicians performing today, plus some talented newcomers. In addition to this September event, Arbuckle Mountain Bluegrass Park hosts the Spring Jam in May and the Fall Jam in October.

★ Czech Festival

This event celebrating Czech culture and traditions is held in Yukon, near Oklahoma City, on the first weekend in October. The festival includes a parade up Main Street, carnival rides, music and dancing, craft displays, and many opportunities to enjoy traditional Czech foods.

★ Poteau Balloon Fest

In Eastern Oklahoma, hot-air balloons hover over the town of Poteau in October. But this festival is more than just balloons. With mud pit races, stagecoach rides, a pet costume contest, skydivers, helicopter rides, a carnival, and American Indian dancers, this event offers something for everyone.

How the Government Works

Oklahoma's constitution was adopted in 1907, when Oklahoma became a state. The constitution and other state laws provide for multiple levels of government. Oklahoma's state government consists of the legislative branch, which passes laws; the executive branch, which carries out the laws; and the judicial branch, which interprets the laws and administers justice. The state has 77 counties, which are divided into townships. State law also provides for the establishment of cities and towns, which have their own local government. Oklahoma's Indian nations choose their own leaders, who work together with state and federal government officials.

In addition to casting votes for state, county, and local officials, Oklahomans vote for president of the United States and for members of the U.S. Congress. The state elects two U.S. senators and five members of the U.S. House of Representatives. In presidential elections since the 1950s, Oklahoma voters have usually favored the Republican Party candidate.

How a Bill Becomes a Law

Most Oklahoma laws start out as bills introduced by a state senator or representative. A bill is a proposed law. The legislator first presents the idea in written form. In most cases, the bill is then sent to a committee in the chamber where it is first introduced. The committee discusses the bill and may make

The legislature meets in the Oklahoma State Capitol building in Oklahoma City. The building opened in 1919, but the present dome was not added until 2002.

Members of the house of representatives gather in this room to discuss and vote on proposed new laws.

changes to it. Lawmakers serve on a variety of committees. Each committee focuses on a specific topic, such as transportation, finance, or the environment. Some committee meetings on a bill may be open to the public. People can attend such meetings and offer their views on the bill, for or against.

If the committee approves the bill, it is sent back to the chamber where it was introduced. The members of that chamber then have the chance to discuss the bill and make further changes. Finally, the bill comes up for a vote. If it passes, the bill goes to the other chamber of the legislature. There, the bill goes through a similar process. It is examined, debated, changed, and brought up for a vote. If the bill fails to pass in the second chamber, it cannot become law.

Often, the version of a bill that passes in the second chamber differs in important ways from the version that passed in the first one. In such cases, the bill is sent to a conference committee in which members of both chambers take part. The committee discusses the measure and works out a compromise version. This version is then submitted to the two separate chambers. If both chambers pass this final bill without further changes, it is sent to the governor. If the governor signs the bill, it then becomes law.

Sometimes, the legislature passes a bill that the governor opposes. In that case, the governor may reject, or veto, the measure. The bill then has one last chance to become law. It is returned to the legislature. If two-thirds of the members of each chamber vote to override the veto, the bill then passes despite the governor's opposition. After final passage, the measure is recorded, printed, and becomes an official part of Oklahoma law.

Initiative and Referendum

Most bills become law by gaining the approval of the legislature and the signature of the governor. But the state constitution offers Oklahomans two other, more direct methods to pass or change state laws. These methods are called initiative and referendum.

The initiative method allows people to propose new laws and constitutional changes, or amendments. Voters may then approve or reject the proposals at the next election. In order to qualify for the ballot, an initiative must receive a certain number of signatures, based on a specific percentage of the number of people who voted for governor at the

Branches of Government

EXECUTIVE ★ ★ ★ ★ ★ ★ ★
The governor heads the state's executive branch. He or she is chosen by the state's voters to serve a four-year term and may serve no more than two terms in a row. Voters also choose key officials who help the governor run the state. They include the lieutenant governor, attorney general, and secretary of state.

LEGISLATIVE ★ ★ ★ ★ ★ ★ ★
Oklahoma's state legislature is made up of two parts, or chambers. The senate has forty-eight members, each elected to a four-year term. The house of representatives is larger, with 101 members serving for two years each. Oklahomans have voted to limit the number of terms that state legislators may serve. Each lawmaker may not serve more than a combined total of 12 years in both houses of the legislature.

JUDICIAL ★ ★ ★ ★ ★ ★ ★
The highest court in the state, the supreme court, has a chief justice and eight other justices. They are appointed by the governor and then approved by the state's voters to their six-year terms. The state also has a court of civil appeals, made up of at least twelve judges, and a court of criminal appeals, with five judges. Lower courts include district courts and municipal courts.

previous election. To win approval, the proposal must be supported by a majority of people voting on that issue on Election Day.

The other method that allows voters to have a direct say in approving or rejecting laws is called a referendum. When the legislature calls for a referendum, it gives voters a chance to accept or reject a new law before it takes effect. Voters may also propose a referendum to reject a law that has already been passed. As with voter initiatives, a certain number of signatures must be collected before a citizen-proposed referendum can get on the ballot. In order to pass, a referendum must gain a majority of those voting on that issue.

County and Local Government

County government in Oklahoma relies on commissioners. Each county is divided into districts, and each district elects a county commissioner. The

Through the initiative process, voters on Election Day can directly approve a new law, bypassing the state legislature.

commissioners work together to make sure county residents have access to services and programs. County residents also elect a sheriff to maintain law and order.

There are almost 600 cities and towns in the state. In each locality, voters usually elect a city or town council. Most cities also elect a mayor or city manager. Cities with a population of more than 2,000 can draw up and amend their own charters. A charter is a document describing how the community is to be run. Each city has its own unique set of needs and problems. By having the power to set their own local laws and rules, the citizens of Oklahoma are able to tackle these concerns directly.

Contacting Lawmakers

★ ★ ★ ★ ★ ★ ★ ★ ★ ★ ★ ★

To find contact information for Oklahoma legislators, go to this website:

http://www.capitolconnect.com/ oklahoma/default.aspx

If you are an Oklahoma resident, enter your address information and click "Submit." The page then displays information about your state and federal legislators.

Quick Facts

GOVERNOR, SENATOR, OIL BARON

Robert S. Kerr was one of the most powerful political and business leaders in Oklahoma's history. Born in 1896 in a log cabin near Ada, Kerr became governor in 1943. He later served fifteen years in the U.S. Senate, where he aided the oil and gas industry. Kerr also helped to develop the dams and waterways that link the Arkansas River to ocean ports.

Making a Living

For much of Oklahoma's history, the economy has risen and fallen based on demand for the state's mineral and agricultural products. Since the 1990s, however, state officials have made a determined effort to broaden the economy. An increasing number of Oklahomans now work in service industries (in which workers provide a service to other people rather than produce things) and in high-tech jobs. Because high-tech jobs require a well-educated workforce, the state is also making efforts to strengthen its educational system. As of 2012, Oklahoma lagged behind the national average in the percentage of adults holding college diplomas and graduate degrees.

Agriculture

Although Oklahoma is known for its oil and natural gas reserves, agriculture is also important to the state. Oklahoma has more than 86,000 farms and ranches, which cover a combined total of about 35 million acres (14.2 million ha). Once, cotton was Oklahoma's chief crop. In recent times, winter wheat has taken its place. Oklahoma currently raises about 5 percent of the nation's annual winter wheat crop.

Oklahoma is a leading producer in many other categories as well. The state ranks among national leaders in the production of pecans, peanuts, rye, grain sorghum, hogs, and cattle and calves. Farms in the Arkansas River valley grow

About 6 million acres (2.4 million ha) of Oklahoma farmland are used for growing winter wheat.

RECIPE FOR A PEACH SMOOTHIE

Peaches are an important crop for many Oklahoma farmers. The following is a recipe that uses fresh peaches to make a tasty drink.

WHAT YOU NEED

2 medium-sized peaches, cut and pitted

1 ripe banana, peeled

5 frozen strawberries

8 ounces (0.25 liter) orange juice or pineapple juice

Have an adult help you cut the peaches and remove the pits. Place the fruit in a blender. Peel the banana and place it in the blender. Add the frozen strawberries to the blender, and pour in the orange juice or pineapple juice.

Have an adult help you blend the ingredients. If the smoothie is too thick, you can add a little more juice. If the smoothie is too thin, you can add a scoop of vanilla ice cream to the blender, replace the top, and turn the blender on for another 20 seconds.

If you have other favorite fruits, such as blueberries, mangoes, papayas, or pineapples, you can substitute one of them for the strawberries and the banana. But some fruits, such as apples or raisins, do not work very well in smoothies. Also, some juices, such as apple juice, do not work as well as others. So ask an adult for advice if you want to add a different kind of fruit or juice to your smoothie. Then, enjoy your refreshing drink.

Raising cattle has been an important part of the Oklahoma economy for a century and a half.

spinach, beans, and carrots. Peach orchards can be found in Eastern and Central Oklahoma, especially around the towns of Porter and Stratford. In the Red River valley, cotton, peanuts, and a range of vegetables are the main crops. Corn and soybeans round out the list of the main foods raised in Oklahoma soil.

The state's most valuable agricultural product is cattle. More than 5 million cattle and calves graze on Oklahoma's grasslands and fatten in the state's many feedlots. Chickens, hogs, dairy cows, and turkeys are also raised on the state's ranches and farms. The combined value of Oklahoma's agricultural production was nearly $6 billion in 2009.

Mining and Energy

Oklahoma's economy in the twentieth century was built on oil. Although the petroleum industry has been less dominant since the 1990s, it is still a major employer statewide. Oil deposits are found in nearly every county in the state. But oil is not the only treasure stored below ground. Natural gas is also found

Workers & Industries

Industry	Number of People Working in That Industry	Percentage of All Workers Who Are Working in That Industry
Education and health care	383,820	23.0%
Wholesale and retail businesses	239,992	14.4%
Publishing, media, entertainment, hotels, and restaurants	190,821	11.4%
Manufacturing	158,890	9.5%
Professionals, scientists, and managers	126,549	7.6%
Construction	115,736	6.9%
Government	104,459	6.3%
Banking and finance, insurance, and real estate	101,266	6.1%
Other services	86,184	5.2%
Transportation and public utilities	85,505	5.1%
Farming, fishing, forestry, and mining	73,382	4.4%
Totals	1,666,604	100%

Notes: Figures above do not include people in the armed forces.
"Professionals" includes people such as doctors and lawyers.
Percentages may not add to 100 because of rounding.

Source: U.S. Bureau of the Census, 2010 estimates

at most of Oklahoma's oil fields. The state has more than 80,000 producing oil wells and more than 40,000 producing gas wells. Each year, as old wells are retired, hundreds of new wells are drilled. The industry directly contributes more than $26 billion annually to the state economy. Oklahoma ranks third among the fifty states in natural gas production and sixth in oil. Pipelines are another source of employment and income. They help move the state's large supply of oil and gas. Workers are needed to build the lines and make sure they are maintained to prevent any possible leaking.

Although oil reigns supreme in the Sooner State, Oklahoma has other valuable mineral resources as well. Rich beds of coal line parts of northeastern and east-central Oklahoma. The state's uplands provide valuable reserves of sand, gravel, limestone, gypsum, and salt. The sand and gravel are used for concrete and for highway construction and repair. Limestone, often in the form of crushed stone, is found in large quarries in the southwestern part of the state. Gypsum is used for construction and for products such as fertilizer.

Oklahoma generates most of its electricity from natural gas and coal. Recently, the state has been developing an energy source that does not come from underground—wind. The first modern wind farm in Oklahoma began producing electricity in 2003. With its great expanses of open prairie, Oklahoma offers excellent conditions for additional wind farm construction, especially in the Panhandle.

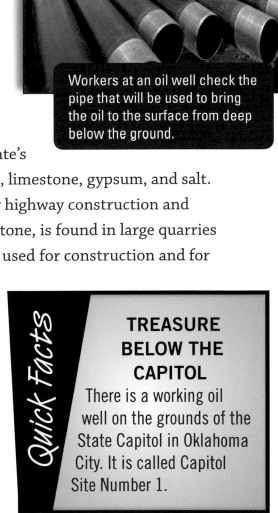

Workers at an oil well check the pipe that will be used to bring the oil to the surface from deep below the ground.

Quick Facts

TREASURE BELOW THE CAPITOL
There is a working oil well on the grounds of the State Capitol in Oklahoma City. It is called Capitol Site Number 1.

Products & Resources

Oil

Over the past century, Oklahoma's economy thrived to a large extent on the strength of its oil reserves. The state's rich oil and natural gas resources helped fuel a growing international energy industry. New technologies to find, pump, and process oil and natural gas were first tested in Oklahoma.

Cattle

Beef cattle are the state's top agricultural earner. From raising the cattle to processing the meat, the cattle industry normally provides many thousands of jobs. The larger cattle operations are usually found in the western part of the state. A severe drought hurt the industry in 2011.

Pecans

The state ranks among U.S. leaders in the production of pecans. The pecan harvest averages about 18 million pounds (8.2 million kg) per year, contributing some $22 million a year, on average, to the state's economy. The 1999 harvest produced a record-breaking 63 million pounds (28.6 million kg). The tasty nuts are sold to companies around the world.

Electronics

Electronic equipment ranks high among the state's manufactured products. Tulsa is a center for the production of aerospace equipment. In Oklahoma City, communications equipment is a major product, while aircraft parts are made in Shawnee.

Wheat

Wheat has long been Oklahoma's most important grain crop. The state's industry received a major boost in the late twentieth century with the opening up of markets in China. In recent years, however, wheat production has declined, as some Oklahoma farmers have planted crops that bring higher prices on world markets.

Eggs

The poultry industry in Oklahoma supplies the state and the nation with chickens and eggs. Each year, state poultry farmers usually market between 750 million and 800 million eggs. Egg production brings Oklahoma more than $80 million in income annually.

Manufacturing

Much of the manufacturing in Oklahoma serves the needs of the state's oil and gas drillers, farmers, and military bases. Many factories produce equipment used by the petroleum industry. Machine parts, construction equipment, and heating and cooling devices are other Oklahoma products.

Factories near many of the state's larger cities turn out high-tech equipment, including motor parts and communication systems used by the U.S. military. Other factories in the state process foods, refine metals, and produce rubber and plastic products. Plants near Tulsa and Oklahoma City assemble cars and trucks and produce equipment for airplanes and spacecraft.

Tourism and Services

Tourism contributes more than $6 billion per year to the Oklahoma economy and provides jobs for about 75,000 state residents. State parks, located throughout Oklahoma, attract more than 12 million visitors per year. Outdoor attractions range from the canyons and ranches of northwestern Oklahoma to the mountains, forests, and scenic waterfalls that mark the southern portion of the state. Also popular with tourists is the city of Tulsa, sometimes called the "oil capital of the world." Two of the city's major attractions are the Gilcrease Museum, which holds an extensive collection of American Indian art and artifacts, and the Philbrook Museum of Art, which has more than 8,500 works in its international collection. The Philbrook is housed in a restored 1920s villa in the heart of the city.

Tulsa's main sports and performing arts arena is the Bank of Oklahoma (BOK) Center, designed by the celebrated modern architect Cesar Pelli. Chesapeake

Sand Creek, popular with visitors who enjoy fishing, flows through Oklahoma's Osage Hills State Park.

OKLAHOMA'S GREATEST ATHLETE

Born in 1887 in a one-room cabin near Prague, Jim Thorpe starred in just about every sport he tried. An Olympic standout in track and field, Thorpe—who was part Indian—also played professional football and baseball. A member of the Pro Football Hall of Fame, he was named by the Associated Press in 1950 as the outstanding athlete of the first half of the twentieth century. He died in 1953.

Energy Arena is the home of the Oklahoma City Thunder of the National Basketball Association. The state's major institutions of higher education include the University of Oklahoma, which has its main campus in Norman, and Oklahoma State University, headquartered in Stillwater. In college sports, the University of Oklahoma Sooners have long been a football powerhouse.

Tourism, education, and the health care industry are major sources of employment for workers in the service sector of Oklahoma's

Kevin Durant (in blue) has been a leading scorer for the Oklahoma City Thunder since joining the team in 2008.

Sooners fans turn out to cheer their favorite college football team, which has won seven national championships since 1950.

economy. Other service employees work in department stores, supermarkets, and other stores, as well as in restaurants and hotels. Some provide fellow Oklahomans with cars, insurance, legal advice, and new homes.

Most service jobs are found in or near Oklahoma's major urban areas. These jobs make up an important part of the state's "new economy" for the twenty-first century.

State Flag & Seal

An Osage shield stands in the center of the blue background on the state's flag. The shield is covered with two symbols of peace. A traditional American Indian peace pipe is crossed by an olive branch. The word "Oklahoma" appears below the many feathers hanging from the shield. The basic design was officially adopted in 1925, and the word "Oklahoma" was added in 1941.

A white star appears in the center of the state seal. In its center, a settler and an American Indian shake hands. They stand for the spirit of peace and cooperation that exists among all the peoples of Oklahoma. On the star's five points are symbols of each of the Five Civilized Tribes brought to the state in the early 1800s. Around the star are forty-five smaller stars. They stand for each of the states that entered the Union before Oklahoma became the forty-sixth state. The seal was adopted in 1907.

OKLAHOMA

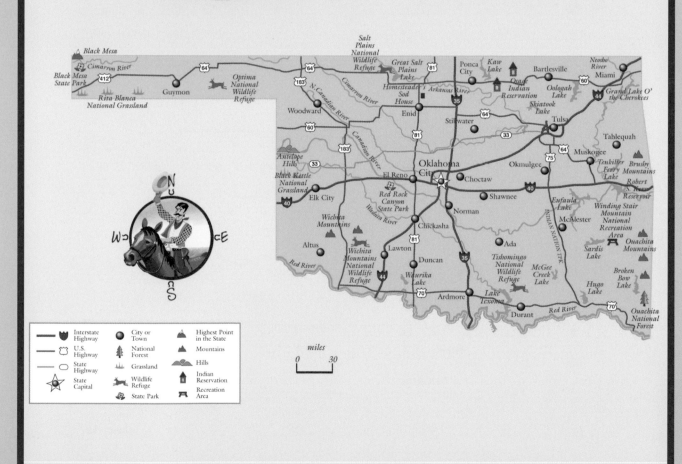

Black Mesa
Black Mesa State Park
Cimarron River
412
Rita Blanca National Grassland
Guymon
64
Optima National Wildlife Refuge
64
183
N. Canadian River
Salt Plains National Wildlife Refuge
Great Salt Plains Lake
81
Ponca City
Kaw Lake
Osage Indian Reservation
Bartlesville
Neosho River
Miami
60
Homesteader's Sod House
Arkansas River
Enid
Stillwater
35
64
Oologah Lake
Skiatook Lake
Tulsa
Grand Lake O' the Cherokees
44
Woodward
Cimarron River
Canadian River
60
183
Antelope Hills
33
Black Kettle National Grassland
40
Elk City
81
81
Oklahoma City
33
Tahlequah
El Reno
Red Rock Canyon State Park
Choctaw
Okmulgee
75
Muskogee
64
Tenkiller Ferry Lake
Brushy Mountains
Robert S. River Reservoir
Wichita Mountains
Washita River
Norman
Shawnee
40
Eufaula Lake
McAlester
Winding Stair Mountain National Recreation Area
Ouachita Mountains
Altus
Wichita Mountains National Wildlife Refuge
Lawton
Chickasha
Duncan
Ada
Tishomingo National Wildlife Refuge
McGee Creek Lake
Sardis Lake
Broken Bow Lake
Red River
Waurika Lake
35
81
INDIAN NATION TPK
Hugo Lake
70
44
Ardmore
Lake Texoma
70
Durant
Red River
70
Ouachita National Forest

miles
0   30

Legend

Interstate Highway	City or Town	Highest Point in the State
U.S. Highway	National Forest	Mountains
State Highway	Grassland	Hills
State Capital	Wildlife Refuge	Indian Reservation
	State Park	Recreation Area

State Song

Oklahoma

words by Oscar Hammerstein II and music by Richard Rodgers

Brand new State! Brand new State! gon - na treat you great! _____ Gon - na give you bar - ley, Car - rots and per - ta - ters, Pas - ture fer the cat - tle, Spin - ach and ter - may - ters! Flow - ers on the prair - ie where the June bugs zoom, Plen' - y of air and plen' - y of room, Plen' - y of room to swing a rope! _____ Plen' - y of heart and plen' - y of hope. _____

CHORUS

O _____ k - la - hom - a, where the

BOOKS

Dorman, Robert L. *It Happened in Oklahoma*. Guilford, CT: Globe Pequot Press, 2011.

Golus, Carrie. *Jim Thorpe*. Minneapolis: Twenty-First Century Books, 2008.

Henningfeld, Diane Andrews (ed.). *The Oklahoma City Bombing* (Perspectives on Modern World History). Detroit: Greenhaven Press, 2012.

Reis, Ronald A. *Mickey Mantle*. New York: Chelsea House, 2008.

WEBSITES

Encyclopedia of Oklahoma History & Culture
http://digital.library.okstate.edu/encyclopedia

Official Oklahoma Tourism Site
http://www.travelok.com

Oklahoma City National Memorial & Museum—Official Website
http://www.oklahomacitynationalmemorial.org

Oklahoma Music Hall of Fame & Museum—Official Website
http://www.omhof.com

Oklahoma's Official Website
http://www.ok.gov

Oklahoma Scenic Rivers—Information for Kids
http://www.oklahomascenicrivers.net/kids.asp

Doug Sanders is a writer and editor who lives in New York City. His favorite places to visit in the Sooner State are the Wichita Mountains and the memorial to the victims of the Oklahoma City bombing.

Geoffrey M. Horn has written more than fifty books for young people and adults, along with hundreds of articles for encyclopedias and other works. He lives in Red Bank, New Jersey, with his wife and three cats, and he has traveled extensively throughout the United States and overseas.

INDEX

Page numbers in **boldface** are illustrations.